The British Airliner Colle

I am very pleased to write this introduction to the collection of twelve British Airliners based at IWM Duxford particularly as this is the first time that a comprehensive guide to the whole collection has been published. The publication of this guide to the collection also marks the launch of its new identity as The British Airliner Collection.

The airliners form an integral part of the huge variety of aircraft exhibits to be seen at Duxford but all are owned and maintained by the Duxford Aviation Society (DAS).

The Society was formed in 1975 by a group of enthusiasts who set themselves the objective of building up a collection of post second world war British civil aircraft. This is now the primary focus of the Society but over the past 35 years volunteer members have played a key role in preserving and restoring the Duxford site itself as it has developed into the world famous museum it is today.

The first aircraft to be acquired by the Society was the De Havilland Comet 4 generously donated by Dan Air and flown to Duxford in February 1974.

This was followed by the Bristol Britannia, donated by Monarch Airlines, in June 1975, again flown into Duxford and then by the Vickers Viscount dismantled by DAS volunteers in Liverpool over a three month period and transported to Duxford by road in 1976.

In 1977 the Department of Industry gifted the pre-production Concorde 101 to the Society. The remaining aircraft were subsequently added to the collection between 1980 and 1993.

The current priority of the Duxford Aviation Society is to restore and maintain the airliner collection in good condition and to use the collection to illustrate the rapid technological developments of the period at a time when British companies led the World in aeronautical engineering.

This booklet gives details of each of the airliners as well as the history and development of the type and it also includes anecdotes and typical experiences of passengers who travelled on the aircraft at the time.

It is intended to produce further booklets explaining the political and commercial pressures that led to the rapid merging of British aircraft companies and the loss of such famous names as De Havilland, Avro, Vickers, Handley Page and Hawker Siddeley.

In the meantime I am sure you will find this booklet a fascinating guide to The British Airliner Collection.

The Duxford Aviation Society is a registered charity and relies on volunteers to carry out restoration, care and maintenance work. All profits from this booklet will go towards the cost of maintaining the collection.

David Garside
Chairman, Duxford Aviation Society
March 2012

Duxford Aviation Society has taken every effort to contact copyright holders of photographs and extracts from personal papers; and seek their permission. We trust we have not infringed any copyright and if so, we apologise and ask that you contact us.

Photograph acknowledgements: Front cover, p10, p39: Reeve Photography, p21: Francois Prins, p28: Ken Pettit, p33: Allen Churchyard.

Avro York G-ANTK

This aircraft served in the Berlin airlift in 1948/9 and carried the 100,000th ton of supplies into Berlin.

The British Airliner Collection's York

The Avro York was a long-range transport that was designed to use the same wings, engines, undercarriage, and tail unit (with a third fin added) as the Lancaster bomber. 'TK was built at Yeadon and was rolled out in January 1946. It entered RAF service with 242 Squadron as MW 232 that August, being based for a time at Oakington. In May 1947 it moved to 511 Squadron at Lyneham, and was used on trooping and cargo flights, including many to the Far East. In 1948/49 it was used on the Berlin Air Lift operation, and suffered an undercarriage collapse during a landing there, in January 1949, but was repaired and put into storage. In 1950/51 it was used

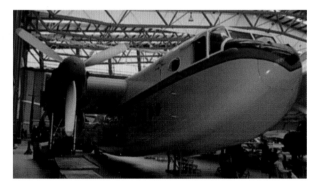

by Fairey Aviation for in-flight refuelling trials before being put back into storage awaiting disposal.

In 1954 it was bought by Dan-Air and registered G-ANTK. It was based firstly at Blackbushe and then at Gatwick, and was used mainly on long-range freight charters to Africa and the Far East, including many flights under an MoD contract to the Woomera Rocket Range in Australia. It was finally retired at Lasham in April 1964. It was fitted with bunks and used for a time by a local Scout group as their headquarters.

In 1974, with the aircraft deteriorating badly through standing outside, a group of Dan-Air engineers began restoring the aircraft in their spare time, but this proved difficult because of the limited time which they could devote to the job, and eventually Dan-Air offered both the York and their Airspeed Ambassador to Duxford Aviation Society on long-term loan for restoration and preservation at Duxford. The York was moved by road to Duxford on 23rd May 1986 and after a complete restoration which took 20 years, it was given an official roll-out before being moved into the new AirSpace building where it is now permanently on display.

A number of items of historical interest are housed in the York. One is a wheel recovered from the York aircraft in which Air Chief Marshal Sir Trafford Leigh-Mallory was killed on 14th November 1944 when en route to Burma to take up the post of Air Commander-in-Chief of South East Asia Command (SEAC). The aircraft crashed in France in bad weather and this wheel was recovered from the crash site. Leigh-Mallory had direct connections with Duxford: during the Battle of Britain he was in command of 12 Group RAF Fighter Command, which included the squadrons based here. There is also a seat used by the late British Prime Minister Harold Wilson (then Secretary for Overseas Trade) when he was flying home from a trade mission to Moscow in 1947. His York aircraft overshot the runway at Heathrow and Mr Wilson was injured in the crash.

Special Yorks

Most Yorks had a solidly unspectacular life as transports and passenger aeroplanes but a few did have slightly more interesting passengers; such as elephants bound for London Zoo!

Churchill's Egg

One of the prototype Yorks, LV633, Ascalon, was custom-built as the personal transport and flying conference room for Prime Minister Winston Churchill. Ascalon was to be fitted with a special pressurized "egg" so that VIP passengers could be carried without their having to use an oxygen mask. Made of aluminium alloy it had eight Perspex windows to reduce claustrophobia. It also had a telephone, instrument panel, drinking facilities and an ashtray with room for cigars, thermos flask, newspapers and books. Testing at RAE Farnborough found the "egg" to work satisfactorily. However, Avro said it was too busy with the new Lancaster IV (Avro Lincoln) work so it was never actually installed in Ascalon. The whereabouts of "Churchill's Egg" is currently unknown.

Australia's only York

MW104, Endeavour, flew to Australia in 1945 to become the personal aircraft of HRH The Duke of Gloucester, Australia's then Governor-General. It was operated by the Governor-General's Flight from 1945 to 1947, and it was the Royal Australian Air Force's only York.

Indian heat

Another York (MW102) was fitted out as a "flying office" for the use of Viceroy of India and C-in-C South East Asia Command, Lord Mountbatten. During its first major overhaul by Avro at Manchester Ringway in 1945, the aircraft was re-painted a light duck egg green, a shade intended to cool down the aeroplane, instead of its former normal camouflage colour scheme.

South African dignitary

South African leader Jan Smuts also used a York as personal transport.

But perhaps most special of all: the Berlin Airlift contribution

During the Berlin Airlift, Yorks flew 58,124 of the 131,800 sorties conducted by the RAF.

On 17th December 1948, the British Airliner Collection's Avro York, then the RAF's MW232, piloted by Flight Lieutenant Beeson airlifted a cargo of canned meat into Gatow. It was the 100,000th ton of provisions brought in by Operation 'Plainfare'.

The last Yorks were retired from service by Skyways and Dan Air in 1964!

THE BRITISH
AIRLINER COLLECTION

De Havilland DH104 Dove G-ALFU

The first British civil transport aircraft produced after WW2.

The British Airliner Collection's Dove

'FU was built as a Dove 4, later being modified to Dove 6 specification with more powerful engines. It spent the whole of its flying career from 1948 to 1972 based at Stansted Airport, and was used by the Civil Aviation Flying Unit for checking airport navigational aids and radio communications, and also for aircrew training. During its long career it flew a total of 10,597 hours. It was donated to the Imperial War Museum and was moved to Duxford in 1973. In February 1984 it was transferred to Duxford Aviation Society.

History and Development

The Dove was the first British aircraft to be produced after WW2, as a light transport aircraft and a replacement for the pre-war D.H. Rapide biplane. It was used by airlines on shorter routes such as those to the Scilly Isles and the Scottish islands, and on feeder routes to the main airports. Many were also used as company transports, while others were also used by the Services for communications work – the RAF called it the Devon and the Navy named theirs the Sea Devon. The total number of Doves built was 544.

The Dove was de Havilland's first postwar civil aircraft and one of the few successful Brabazon Committee projects, with the prototype flying just six weeks after the Japanese surrender.

The Brabazon Committee was established in 1942 to define requirements for British postwar civil aircraft and although responsible for a number of failures such as the Bristol Brabazon, its studies also resulted in the highly successful Vickers Viscount (described elsewhere) and the de Havilland Dove.

The Dove was developed in response to a requirement for a small feederliner for UK and Commonwealth domestic services. The resulting aircraft featured new versions of the Gipsy Queen engine, a raised flightdeck and separate passenger cabin and all metal construction. The first DH.104 Dove flew for the first time on 25th September 1945.

The Dove remained in production until the mid-1960s (by which time it was a Hawker Siddeley product), and a number of variants were built. These were the initial Series 1, the executive interior Series 2, the military Series 4, the Series 5 with greater range and more powerful engines, the Series 6 (and 6A for the USA) executive version of the Series 5, Series 6BA with more powerful engines, Series 7 (Series 7A for the USA) with more powerful engines and raised Heron style flightdeck, and Series 8 (8A or Custom 800 in the USA) with five seat interior.

De Havilland Dove: a Traveller's Tale

In complete contrast to the British Airliner Collection's Dove, which spent its entire life based at Stansted flying for the Civil Aviation Authority some Doves had a much more colourful life. Below is the story of one such aeroplane; it's eventual recovery and restoration also stands as a testament to the dedicated staff and volunteers of the SAA Museum; an organisation dedicated to the preservation of that country's civil aviation heritage.

The de Havilland DH 104 Dove, de Havilland's first post-war production aircraft, was developed to replace the de Havilland DH 89 Dragon Rapide. Development began in 1944 and the aircraft was of all metal construction with a semi-monocoque fuselage structure covered with a stressed aluminium skin. South African Airways purchased two of these eight-seat British-built aircraft for use on the proposed feeder services in South Africa.

> The Dove was de Havilland's first postwar civil aircraft, and one of the few successful Brabazon Committee projects. The prototype first flew in 1945.

The story of ZS-BCC

The delivery flight from 5th-14th December 1947 was an event in itself: UK-Paris-Dijon-Geneva-Rome-Malta-Tripoli-El Adem-Wadi Halfa-Khartoum-Juba-Kisumu-Tabora-Ndola-Salisbury-and eventually Johannesburg.

It operated its first service from Johannesburg on 8th March 1948 to Windhoek, via Kimberley, Upington, Karasburg and Keetmanshoop. Utilisation was, however, very low. And when ZS-BCC operated its last service from Lourenco Marques to Johannesburg on 30th October 1951, it had only 307 hours on the clock.

It was sold and delivered to Northern Rhodesia (Zambia) as VP-RCL on 18th March 1952. It was operated by Northern Rhodesia Aviation Services for several years. The aircraft also belonged to Anglo-American at one time before becoming 9J-RHX on 15 February 1968 with Mines Air Services, still in Zambia.

Only a few months later, on 27th March 1968 it was acquired by Fairey Surveys in England as G-AWFM and after an uneventful return to these shores it was modified for use in photographic surveys with a large camera hatch in the aft cabin, and the non-standard cockpit top. During its time with Fairey, G-AWFM's logbook shows such destinations as Ajaccio, Tripoli and Jeddah, whilst its home base was White Waltham airfield near Maidenhead, Berkshire.

Death and Rebirth

In January 1976 it was finally withdrawn from service, and left to rot in the open, but several years later it was offered to and acquired by South African Airways (SAA).

Transportation to South Africa was the next hurdle to be overcome. Shipment by sea was the obvious solution, but preparation and crating charges proved prohibitive. The only alternative was for it to be dismantled and accommodated in "conventional" aircraft.

The Dove was disassembled and moved to Salisbury Hall, the home of the Mosquito Museum, for storage. The first sections left for Johannesburg in the cargo hold of an SAA 747. On 12th February 1979 it arrived back in South Africa, some 27 years after leaving.

After being restored by the SAA apprentice school the aircraft is now part of the SAA Museum Society collection at Rand Airport and wears post war livery.

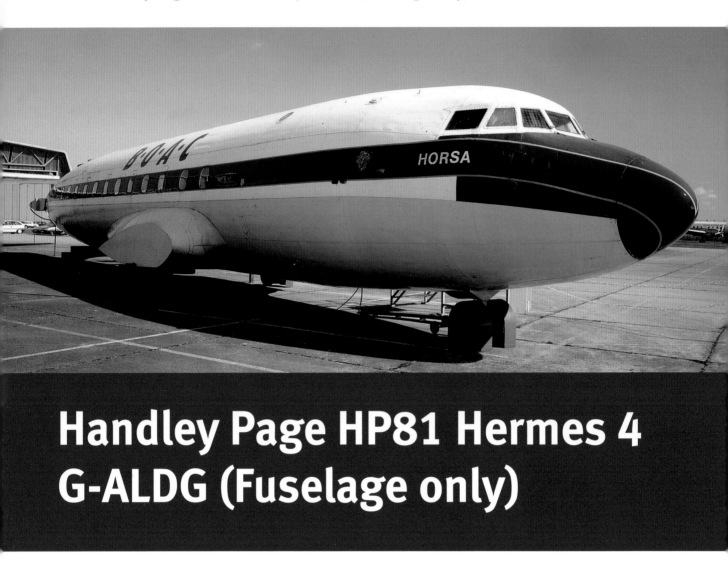

Handley Page HP81 Hermes 4 G-ALDG (Fuselage only)

The only surviving Hermes, the interior is an exhibition devoted to its manufacturer, Handley Page.

The British Airliner Collection's Hermes

'DG was delivered to BOAC in 1950, which operated it until 1953. The following year it was sold to Airwork, then to Falcon Airways, and then to Silver City, who all used it on holiday charter and trooping flights until 1962, when it was retired at Gatwick to be scrapped. The fuselage survived, and was used by British Caledonian for cabin crew training, before being passed to the Gatwick Fire Service who used it for smoke evacuation training. When they had no further use for it they appealed for an aircraft preservation group to rescue it, as it was the only surviving part of a Hermes, and eventually the Duxford Aviation Society and the Handley Page Association jointly arranged for it to be moved by road to Duxford. This took place in January 1981 and restoration of the interior of the fuselage began. This took until 2006 to finally complete, and the Hermes is now on display in AirSpace.

Part of the interior is an exhibition devoted to the aircraft and its manufacturer, Handley Page. A small section of the cabin has also been fitted with replica seating to show what it would have been like to travel on board this aircraft.

History and Development

The Hermes was the first large passenger aircraft to be built in Britain after the end of WW2, and the first to be pressurised. The original Hermes was similar in design to the company's Hastings military transport, but it was later redesigned with a tricycle undercarriage replacing the original tailwheel. 25 were built for BOAC for use on its West African and South African routes, but in the event only 19 went to BOAC and the others were taken by independent charter-flight operators. The Hermes was a pleasant aircraft to fly on and quite popular with passengers, but it suffered from severe engine problems, mainly because BOAC uprated its Hercules piston engines for operations to high altitude South African airports, and this put additional strains on them, and there were also several incidents where propellers came off in flight. Eventually BOAC replaced the Hermes with the more reliable Canadair Argonaut. They were stored awaiting disposal, but some were later brought back into service when two of BOAC's new Comet 1 Jetliners suffered fatal accidents in similar circumstances and all Comets were grounded.

Once BOAC had finally withdrawn all its Hermes fleet many of them were snapped up by indepentent airlines such as Skyways and Airwork where they gave many years sterling service.

26 May 1952 - Hermes IV G-ALDN (Horus), operated by BOAC, en route from Tripoli, Libya, to Kano, Nigeria, flew off-course for several hours and ran out of fuel, force landing in the Sahara Desert. The passengers and crew all survived the crash and spent several days in the desert, making their way to an oasis and eventual rescue. Pieces recovered from the crashed aeroplane are on view in G-ALDG 'Horsa' located in Airspace.

A Flight on a Hermes

This wonderfully evocative diary extract shows just what travelling on a BOAC Hermes was like in the 1950's. Horus, the Hermes flown on by Mrs Jefferies, was the aeroplane that crashed a few months later in the Sahara desert and is the subject of several display cases in the fuselage of the Collection's Hermes, G-ALDG, Horsa.

Trip to Nigeria 1951

A Diary by A. Margaret Jefferies (1912-1992)

Afternoon tea was served and cigarettes distributed by stewards at intervals. Dinner, preceded by sherry, was served after dark.

Cold soup

Egg mayonnaise

Chop with new potatoes and peas

Strawberries and cream

Cheese and biscuits

Fruit dessert

Coffee

Wine was served with the meal.

The Journey. 1951 Saturday July 21st

Arrived at Airways Terminal Victoria at mid-day, checked in and had lunch on premises:-

Chilled Melon

Roast chicken, new potatoes and peas.

Neapolitan ice-cream.

2pm Boarded coach for Heath Row airport. Passed through customs and were on board B.O.A.C. Hermes "Horus" by 3pm.

Just as we were comfortably settled we were told there was a slight mechanical defect which must be seen to before taking off, so we disembarked and a coach took us back to "Departures" where cups of tea were served.

Passengers who went to greet friends in Spectators' Enclosure saw the Duke of Edinburgh arrive, met by Prince Charles.

Re-embarked, but found two passengers missing and had to wait while they were rounded up. They had been watching the unloading of Prince Philip's luggage which filled 2 vans so evidently he exceeded the regulation 66 lbs!

Took off about one and half hours behind schedule. Fastened seat belts for take-off and stewardess distributed barley sugar and later, when we were airborne, iced lemon squash.

Passed over Epsom and crossed coast just east of Brighton which we identified by its two piers.

Reached French Coast near Dieppe. Very good visibility all the way over France. Picked out rivers Seine and Rhone looking rather like wide satin hair ribbon. Saw Marseilles to east as we crossed the Mediterranean coast.

Flew over a corner of Sardinia, but clouds obscured it. On to North Africa as sun was setting in spectacular shades of electric blue, green, and flame.

Flight very smooth indeed, less sick-making than a motor coach. Seats well sprung, upholstered in blue, mine immediately behind wings, travelling backwards and facing passengers seated behind us, across a fixed table. Other seats faced back of seats in front and had folding tables. Powder room at tail of aircraft had cleansing lotion, make-up base, colognes, hand lotion etc. provided for our use, Elizabeth Arden.

Landed at Castel Benito Airport, Tripoli, about 10:30pm.

Italian and Arab waiters served tea, biscuits, and wine.

Took off after an hour's stop for refuelling for hop over desert to Kano. Take-offs and landings much smoother than I had imagined; we felt no discomfort from change in altitude, though some passengers yawned widely or swallowed violently to relieve ear pressures.

Lights were extinguished in aircraft for night flight but most people slept little owing to sitting-up posture and vibration.

Morning tea dispensed at 4:45. Landed at Kano Northern Nigeria for breakfast at 5:30. Black stewards waited on us with more zeal than efficiency. Had not realised that black men's hands have pink palms and finger tips and that the soles of their feet are pink.

After breakfast, sun had risen. Bright morning with cool breeze. Rest House had some attractive flower beds with zinnias and petunias as well as native plants and shrubs. One shrub had vivid flame red flowers and looked rather like a Christmas tree with bright red luggage labels tied all over it.

Took off at 7:20am. Visibility good at first. Saw Niger and its confluence with Kaduna River then clouds thickened. Clear over Lagos Airport and we landed with no delay, ¾ hour ahead of schedule. We had flown at about 12,000 to 13,000 feet, but pressure inside aircraft was no more than 3,500 feet.

1951, Sunday July 22. Arrival.

T. had set out in good time to meet me and arrived just as the aircraft taxied in. He filled in an immigration form for me to save time so that I got well to the front of the queue through the Customs. The African Customs man looked suspiciously at my travelling case and made me open it for inspection. He showed great interest in the contents of my bottles and jars and seemed to suspect that the Cosmedia lotion might be whiskey. I was tempted to offer him a taste.

Mrs Jefferies continued to note her experiences in Nigeria; a glimpse of a bygone age!

With acknowledgement and thanks to David Jefferies.

Airspeed Ambassador 2 G-ALZO

The only surviving example, now nearing the end of a long-term restoration programme

The British Airliner Collection's Airspeed Ambassador

This airframe is the sole survivor of the production run of 23 Ambassadors built specifically for BEA, who flew them under the name of "Elizabethan".

G-ALZO was delivered to BEA on 25th November 1952, who named it "RMA Christopher Marlowe". It was operated by BEA until June 1958, then it was stored at Cambridge awaiting disposal. In 1960 it was purchased by the Jordanian Air Force for use on VIP and transport flights, based at Amman. In 1963 it was purchased by Dan-Air and was used to carry both passengers and freight, having been fitted with a rear fuselage cargo door by Marshall of Cambridge. On 28th September 1971 it flew from Jersey to Gatwick, the last scheduled flight operated by an Ambassador, and the next day it flew from Gatwick to Rheims and back on a special charter flight. Its last commercial flight was to Zagreb on 2nd October with a replacement engine for a BAC 1-11, returning the following day. It was then retired to the Dan-Air maintenance base at Lasham. It remained there until 1986 when it was donated to the DAS, and it was dismantled and transported by road to Duxford. Its long-term restoration then began and this is still continuing.

History and Development

The prototype Ambassador flew for the first time on 10th July 1947, and was one of the earliest British airliners to have cabin pressurisation.

It had its origin in 1943 as a requirement identified by the Brabazon Committee for a twin-engined, short to medium-haul replacement for the Douglas DC-3.

The design offered seating for 47 passengers and, having a nose wheel undercarriage, looked more modern than the Dakotas, Lancastrians and Vikings that were common on Europe's shorter airline routes. Great efforts were made to reduce drag, to improve performance and enhance cruising efficiency.

The second Ambassador prototype was used by the Bristol Aeroplane Company for the flight testing of the Proteus turboprop engine, later used in the Britannia.

British European Airways (BEA) placed a £3 million order for 20 aircraft in September 1948, and operated them between 1952 and 1958, calling them their "Elizabethan Class" in honour of the newly crowned Queen. The flagship of the fleet was G-ALZN, appropriately named "RMA Elizabethan". The first "Elizabethan" scheduled flight was from Heathrow to Paris Le Bourget on 13th March 1952. After disposal by BEA in 1958, the type helped to establish the scheduled and charter flight operations of Dan-Air, an important airline in the development of package holidays.

In a neat link to another airliner in the Collection the second Ambassador prototype was used by the Bristol Aeroplane Company from 1953 for the flight testing of the Proteus turbo-prop engine; the powerplant of the Britannia.

Manchester United's and Airspeed's darkest day

The Airspeed Ambassador was an unremarkable, but successful airliner that gave many years trouble-free service. It was a solidly unspectacular aeroplane that did its job very well indeed, without fuss, drama, or anything untoward. However it will always be remembered, not for the many years solid service for which it was designed but rather for two spectacular crashes; the 1968 BKS Air Transport Heathrow crash, when, due to a mechanical failure, the aeroplane veered off its landing path and crashed killing all but two of its crew and several of the horses it was transporting, and the Munich Air Disaster ten years earlier. In a career spanning nearly 20 years (the Ambassador entered service in 1952) it is unfortunate that the aeroplane is now mostly remembered for the crashes.

The Munich air disaster: Manchester United's and Airspeed's darkest day.

The Munich air disaster occurred on 6th February 1958, when British European Airways Flight 609 crashed on its third attempt to take off from a slush-covered runway at Munich-Riem Airport in Munich, West Germany. On board the plane was the Manchester United football team, nicknamed the "Busby Babes", along with a number of supporters and journalists.

Takeoff Attempts 1 & 2

The team was returning from a European Cup match in Belgrade, Yugoslavia, against Red Star Belgrade, but had to make a stop in Munich for refuelling, as a non-stop trip from Belgrade to Manchester was out of the Ambassador's range. After refuelling, the pilots, Captains James Thain and Kenneth Rayment, attempted to take off twice, but had to abandon both attempts due to boost surging in the port engine. Fearing that they would get too far behind schedule, Captain Thain rejected an overnight stay in Munich in favour of a third take-off attempt after being advised that opening the throttle more slowly would prevent the surge. They were also of the opinion that the runway was long enough for the slower acceleration.

> "Manchester United goalkeeper Harry Gregg remained behind to pull survivors from the wreckage."

The Fatal 3rd Attempt

By the time of the third attempt, it had begun to snow, but unbeknown to the pilots and ground authorities a layer of slush began to build up at the end of the runway. When the aircraft hit the slush, it lost velocity, making take-off impossible. The aeroplane skidded off the end of the runway and, out of control, crashed into the fence surrounding the airport and then across a road before its port wing was torn off as it caught a house, home to a family of six. The right side of the fuselage hit a wooden hut, inside which was a truck filled with tyres and fuel, which exploded. Fearing that the aircraft might explode, Captain Thain set about getting the surviving passengers as far away as possible. Despite this, Manchester United goalkeeper Harry Gregg remained behind to pull survivors from the wreckage. Twenty of the 44 people on board the aircraft died in the crash. The injured, some of whom had been knocked unconscious, were taken to the Rechts der Isar Hospital in Munich where three more died, resulting in a total of 23 fatalities with 21 survivors.

The Investigation

An investigation by the West German airport authorities originally blamed Captain Thain for the crash, claiming that he had failed to de-ice the wings of the aircraft, despite statements to the contrary from eyewitnesses. It was later established that the crash had, in fact, been caused by the build-up of slush on the runway, which had resulted in the aircraft being unable to achieve take-off velocity; Thain's name was eventually cleared in 1968, ten years after the incident.

Vickers V701 Viscount G-ALWF

The world's first turboprop powered airliner, this is the second production aircraft and the oldest surviving Viscount.

The British Airliner Collection's Viscount

G-ALWF was the second production Viscount, and was part of an order for 20 of the type placed by British European Airways, the initial customer for the aircraft, in August 1950. BEA's aircraft were designated type V.701s, and the order was later increased to 27. The first 20 aircraft were delivered between January 1953 and March 1954, and the additional 7 were delivered between October 1954 and July 1956.

'WF made its first flight at Weybridge on 3rd December 1952. It was registered to BEA on 2nd January 1953 and delivered to the airline on 2nd

February 1953, receiving its Certificate of Airworthiness a week later. BEA named its Viscounts the Discovery Class, and 'WF was named "RMA Sir John Franklin". Over the next two months it was used for crew training and route proving flights, before scheduled services from Heathrow to Cyprus (Nicosia) via Rome and Athens commenced on 18th April with G-AMNY. These were the world's first regular scheduled services using turboprop aircraft, and 'WF operated the second one. The Viscounts were initially fitted with 40 seats in a four-abreast (2 + 2) all-first class layout. They could also accommodate 47 seats in a tourist class layout.

On 12th December 1954 'WF suffered damage to its starboard main undercarriage leg, flaps and

propellers while engaged in crew training at Blackbushe when the undercarriage leg collapsed during a landing. The aircraft was repaired, and returned to service in May 1955. This was a problem with the V.700s and several of BEA's aircraft suffered similar accidents. In the same year the early V.701s were converted to V.701As to bring them up to the same standard as the later aircraft produced for BEA's V.701 order, with Dart 506 engines replacing the original Dart 505s.

In 1959 it was fitted with integral airstairs and an additional port side rear cabin window to allow the passenger area to be extended, allowing it to be operated with a five abreast (2 + 3) 60-63 seat high density passenger seat layout. In 1960 BEA adopted a new red, white and black livery, called the 'Red

Square' livery as it featured the letters BEA in white on a red square background which was incorporated in the black fuselage cheat line and on the white tail fin, and 'WF was repainted in these colours.

From the beginning of 1957 BEA had been taking delivery of its larger and more powerful Viscount V.802s, and the early V701s were disposed of during late 1962 and 1963, with 'WF being sold to Channel Airways. on 6th December 1963. It was leased by Tradair, which was owned by Channel, on 13th March 1964, and was delivered to Southend Airport on 31st of that month. On 18th November 1964 it was flown from Southend to Liverpool on lease to British Eagle International Airlines in the colours of the new operator, who gave it the name "City of Exeter". The lease ended on 26th May 1965 and 'WF was returned to Channel Airways. It operated another flight for British Eagle out of Heathrow on 17th June 1965.

On 15th December 1965 it was sold to Cambrian Airways and was flown to Rhoose Airport, Cardiff, where it was based for the next six years. It was re-registered to Cambrian on 18th January 1966.

'WF's last revenue service took place on 24th December 1971, when it flew from Cardiff to Belfast via Bristol and return, and it was then stored at Rhoose. Because it was by then the oldest Viscount in existence efforts were made by Cambrian to have it preserved, and it was eventually decided that it would be donated to the Viscount Preservation Trust and be displayed to the public at Liverpool Airport. 'WF made its final flight from Rhoose to Liverpool, calling at Heathrow en route to collect dignitaries on 12th April 1972, and it was then officially withdrawn from use. It had then flown a total of 28,299 hours and made 25,938 landings, and had flown almost 7 million miles, carrying an estimated 800,000 passengers. Its registration was cancelled on 18th April 1972.

Under an arrangement between the Trust and the Liverpool Council 'WF was accommodated at the back of No. 1 hangar at Speke Airport, Liverpool, which was the airport's main maintenance hangar. The aircraft was officially opened for viewing by the public from 5th December 1972, but this necessitated the public being allowed into an otherwise restricted area. The aircraft was popular with visitors, with some 4,000 people having walked through it, until, following the introduction of new security regulations, the arrangement had to be ended.

Eventually Duxford Aviation Society offered to dismantle 'WF and move it to Duxford to ensure its continued existence. A team of around twelve DAS volunteers made the 200-mile journey to Liverpool every weekend for three months from November 1975 until January 1976 to dismantle the aircraft. By 14th/15th February the aircraft had been taken apart and it was loaded onto trailers for the journey to its new home. Its fuselage was transported to Duxford by road on 22nd February, followed later by the other main components.

The main job of re-assembling 'WF was carried out in the open as there was no suitable covered accommodation available, commencing in 1976. The missing items from when the aircraft had been used as a source of spares for other Viscounts while it was at Speke had to be sourced and acquired. Replacement time-expired outer wings were obtained courtesy of the airline Alidair. The refurbishment, both external and internal, by the aircraft's small but dedicated team continued over the years through the 1980s. The treatment of external corrosion, a legacy from when it was exposed for two years or so to the

salty air of the Mersey estuary while it was outside at Speke, was a priority. The Cambrian markings were replaced by 'WF's original BEA markings. This was completed by mid-1986.

On 25th November 1992 'WF was put into Hangar 2 and jacked up to allow work to be done to repair and refurbish its main undercarriage. Components including the propellers, engine cowlings and other panels and fairings were removed to allow access to the main structure for some badly-needed refurbishment. Some components were replaced by spare ones donated by various companies, including British Air Ferries and Thameside Aero Spares.

On 21st April 'WF moved into Hangar 1 for repainting. The repainting work began on 1st July and 'WF was finally rolled out of the Hangar on 17th August 1994. Work has continued on 'WF as she stands on the Flightline; most recently by refurbishing the propellers.

On 26th November 2011, the Viscount Preservation Trust handed over the Viscount to the British Airliner Collection for long-term preservation.

The Secret of the Viscount's Success: the Rolls-Royce Dart Turbo-Prop Engine

The Dart is the name of a smooth-flowing, fast-running English river, and Rolls-Royce named their first and most unique engine after it - unique for two reasons, firstly because it was the first turbine in the world to drive a civil aircraft, and secondly on account of its striking simplicity.

To use the words of Rolls-Royce; "Pride of place in any history of the Dart must, of course, be given to the Vickers Viscount because, almost certainly, the engine would never have been developed but for the requirements of this family of aircraft."

Concept

Initially it was proposed that the engine should develop 1000 shaft horsepower through a tractor airscrew and be fitted to a new RAF training aircraft.

The team of designers and draughtsmen were based in the Elton Road office block of Rolls-Royce in Derby under the leadership of Lionel Haworth who was an engineering graduate from the University of Cape Town, South Africa.

Initial detail drawings were issued to the production department on 1st November 1945 and the final build of the RB.53 prototype as it was originally designated was completed on 10th July 1946; an incredibly short design and build time for such a revolutionary engine.

Development did not go smoothly, as when the RDa1, as it was now known, was initially weighed it was found to be overweight at over 1100 lbs, against a target weight of 850 lbs. The oppositions Mamba weighed in at a mere 707 lbs., so Rolls-Royce had to rethink the whole design, if they were to remain competitive.

Civil Development Spurs Progress

Whilst the power development programme was continuing to reach the 1000 shaft horsepower target, Rolls-Royce received a new requirement from the Ministry of Supply to produce a new variant of

the Dart for the proposed Vickers-Armstrong Viceroy (later re-named Viscount) with an increase in power to 1400 shaft horsepower. The increase in power proposed actually helped Rolls-Royce as the power to weight ratio improved.

In 1948 the Viscount prototype (G-AHRF) was fitted with Mark 503 Dart which produced 1250 shaft horsepower. During the first ten months a total of 750 hours flying was carried out, giving Rolls-Royce a lot of data to work with.

An Airspeed Ambassador was also fitted with Dart engines. A water spray rig was fitted to the forward port fuselage to allow icing trials, which resulted in several engine modifications to prevent the hazardous build-up of ice.

Production Viscounts, which were much larger than the prototype, were originally fitted with either the Mark 505 engines or the Mark 506 engines producing up to 1400 shaft horsepower, which became the standard engine on the BEA 700 series fleet. Even more powerful Darts were used in the 800 series Viscounts.

Sadly, the Viscount is extinct operationally, but the Dart soldiers on in the Fokker F27 Friendship, BAe 748, Gulfstream G159, NAMC YS-11 and a few Convair 600 and 640 aircraft.

Evocative Memories

Rolls-Royce may never have expected the Dart to soldier on into the 21st Century, but they are probably not surprised that it has become one of the safest and most reliable engines of its class. The sound of the Dart will always remain memorable to most people who have stood and watched the numerous aircraft that this incredible engine was fitted to, taxying round national and regional airports throughout the world.

De Havilland DH106 Comet 4 G-APDB

This actual aircraft operated the first scheduled service from New York to London by a jet airliner, on 4th October 1958

The British Airliner Collection's Comet 4

Delta Bravo was built at Hatfield as the second of a batch of 19 Comet 4s ordered by BOAC in 1955. It made its maiden flight on 27th July 1958, and on completion of its production test flying was delivered to Heathrow on 12th September 1958. It was used for crew training before being officially handed over to BOAC with its sister aircraft G-APDC on 30th September. The Comet 4s' Certificate of Airworthiness had been issued the previous day. After making a positioning flight to New York 'DB made aviation history on 4th October when it operated the first scheduled service by a jet-powered airliner from New York to London, in the then record time of 6 hours 11 minutes. At the same time 'DC flew

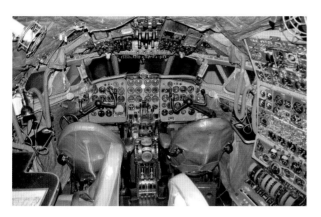

in the opposite direction, from London to New York, the two Comets passing each other in mid-Atlantic when congratulatory radio messages were exchanged. The westbound flight against the prevailing wind took 'DC a total of 10 hours and 13 minutes, including a refuelling stop at Gander. The Comets were fitted with 16 deluxe seats and 32 first-class seats. Just 22 days later Pan American put its new American-built Boeing 707-120s into service on the New York to Paris route. Also in 1958 'DB was used by the Duke of Edinburgh as his personal aircraft for his tour of Canada.

Although not designed specifically to operate on the north Atlantic route, having insufficient range for non-stop flights in both directions with a full payload, BOAC's Comets continued to serve on that route until mid-1960, when the Corporation's new long-range Boeing 707-436s took over. The Comet 4s then flew on services to Africa, India, Australia, South America and the West Indies, fitted with 20 first class and 48 tourist class seats. This was later increased to 81 seats in a five-abreast layout. BOAC finally retired its Comets in 1965.

'DB was sold to Malaysian Singapore Airlines in September 1965 and arrived at its new base, Singapore, on 13th September, where it was re-registered 9M-AOB. It was used by Malaysian Singapore Airlines on both regional and intercontinental routes, including those to Europe, for four years until 11th September 1969, when it was bought by the British independent airline Dan-Air Services. It arrived at Dan-Air's engineering base at Lasham on 16th September, reverting to its original British registration. Based at Gatwick, 'DB was used mainly on inclusive tour holiday flights, carrying up to 106 passengers, but on shorter routes. Its last commercial flight was on 12th November 1973, from Alicante to Tees-side Airport, and it was then retired to Lasham. In view of its interesting history the

directors of Dan-Air decided that it should not be scrapped and it was generously donated to the then East Anglian Aviation Society at Duxford for preservation. 'DB made its last flight on 12th February 1974, making a low pass at Hatfield from where it had made its maiden flight some fifteen years earlier. When it arrived at Duxford it had flown a total of 36,269 hours and made 15,733 landings. It flew more hours than any other Comet. When the Duxford Aviation Society was formed in 1975, 'DB became the first aircraft in its collection of post-WW2 British-built civil aircraft.

History and Development

The Comet 4 was a further improvement on the stretched Comet 3 with even greater fuel capacity. The design had progressed significantly from the original Comet 1, growing by 18ft 6in (5.64 m) and typically seating 74 to 81 passengers compared to the Comet 1's 36 to 44. The Comet 4 was considered the definitive series, having a longer range, higher cruising speed and higher maximum take-off weight. These improvements were possible largely because of Avon engines with twice the thrust of the Comet 1's Ghosts.

BOAC ordered 19 Comet 4s in March 1955, with G-APDA first flying on 27th April 1958. Deliveries to the airline began on 30th September 1958 with two 48-seat aircraft.

The Comet 4 received a welcome response from crews and passengers but was not so well liked by the baggage handlers. The baggage/cargo holds had doors directly underneath the aircraft, so each item of baggage or cargo had to be loaded upwards from the top of the cab of the baggage truck, through the little hole, then slid along the hold floor to be stacked inside. Likewise, the individual pieces of luggage and cargo had to be retrieved slowly and with great effort on arrival!

A Pioneer Aeroplane

The de Havilland DH 106 Comet was the world's first successful commercial jet airliner. Developed and manufactured by de Havilland at Hatfield, Hertfordshire, it first flew in 1949 and was a landmark in aeronautical design. It featured an extremely aerodynamically clean design with its four de Havilland Ghost turbojet engines buried into the wings, a low-noise pressurised cabin, and large windows. When it went into service with BOAC on 2nd May 1952, the Comet was the most exhaustively tested airliner in history. For the era, it was an exceptionally comfortable design and showed signs of being a major success.

The Beginning of the End

The Comet was such a sensation the Queen Mother and Princess Margaret flew in one from London to Rhodesia. By 1953, Britain seemed poised to dominate commercial aviation for the next forty years. As the editor of American Aviation Magazine said, "Whether we like it or not, the British are giving the U.S. a drubbing in jet transport." And then the accidents began.

On 10th January 1954, 20 minutes after taking off from Ciampino, Comet G-ALYP, BOAC Flight 781, broke up in flight and crashed into the Mediterranean off the Italian island of Elba, with the loss of all 35 on board. Engineers at de Havilland immediately recommended 60 modifications aimed at any possible design flaw while the Abell Committee formed to determine potential causes of the crash.

The Second Disaster

On 8th April 1954, Comet G-ALYY, on charter to South African Airways, was on a leg from Rome to Cairo (of a longer flight from London to Johannesburg), when it

> " Britain seemed poised to dominate commercial aviation for the next forty years. "

too crashed in the waters near Naples. The type's Certificate of Airworthiness was immediately revoked; production was suspended at Hatfield while the BOAC fleet was again grounded.

Investigators under the leadership of Sir Arnold Hall, Director of the RAE at Farnborough, began considering fatigue as the most likely cause of both accidents and initiated further research into measurable strain on the skin. With the recovery of large sections of G-ALYP from the Elba crash and the use of G-ALYU, a grounded airframe in an extensive "water torture" test, the RAE hoped for conclusive results.

The Investigation

They built a tank large enough to hold a Comet. The wings protruded from water-tight slots in the sides of the tank. Then the tank and cabin were flooded with water. The water pressure inside the cabin would be raised to eight and a quarter pounds per square inch to simulate the pressure encountered by a Comet at 35,000 feet. It would be held there for three minutes and then lowered while the wings were moved up and down by hydraulic jacks. The hydraulic jacks would simulate the flexing that naturally occurs in aircraft wings during flight. This process continued non-stop, 24 hours a day. This torture test continued until the cabin in the tank had been subjected to the stresses equivalent to 9,000 hours of actual flying. Suddenly, the pressure dropped. The water was drained and the fuselage examined. The investigators were horrified to find a split in the fuselage. It began with a small fracture in the corner of an escape hatch window and extended for eight feet. Metal fatigue! Had the Comet not been under water, the cabin would have exploded like a bomb.

Metal Fatigue, Cracks and Square Windows

By now the RAE engineers had reconstructed about ⅔ of G-ALYP at Farnborough and found fatigue crack growth from a rivet hole at the low-drag fiberglass forward "window" around the Automatic Direction Finder. The crack had spread and caused a catastrophic breakup of the aircraft in high altitude flight.

Stress around the window corners was found to be much higher than expected, and stresses on the skin were generally more than previously expected or tested. This was due to stress concentration, a consequence of the windows' square shape, the levels of stress at these corners could be two or three times that across the rest of the fuselage.

The investigation closed on 24th November 1954. Although they "found that the basic design of the Comet was sound", nonetheless, de Havilland began a refit programme that involved strengthening the fuselage and wing structure, employing thicker gauge skin and replacing all square windows and panels with rounded ones.

Further Development

As is often the case in aeronautical engineering, other aircraft manufacturers learned from, and profited by, de Havilland's hard-learned lessons. Although the Comet had been subjected to the most rigorous testing of any contemporary airliner, the dynamic stresses of pressurisation were not well known, and the Comet had pushed 'the state-of-the-art' beyond its limits. According to John Cunningham, de Havilland's Chief Test Pilot, representatives from American manufacturers such as Boeing and Douglas (privately) "admitted that if it hadn't been for our [de Havilland's] problems, it would have happened to one of them".

Rival manufacturers meanwhile developed their own aircraft and heeded the lessons learnt from the Comet.

Return to Success

The Comet did not resume commercial airline service until 1958. Following the structural problems of the early series, all remaining Comets were withdrawn from service, with de Havilland launching a major effort to build a new version that would be both larger and stronger. The square windows of the Comet 1 were replaced by the oval versions used on the Comet

2, which first flew in 1953, and the skin sheeting was thickened slightly. All production Comet 2s were modified to alleviate the fatigue problems and most of these served with the RAF as the Comet C2. Development flying and route proving with the Comet 3 allowed BOAC to accelerate the certification of what was destined to be the most successful variant of the type. On 24th September 1958, the Comet 4 received its Certificate of Air Worthiness and, the next day, BOAC took delivery of its first two Comet 4s.

And Finally

Dan-Air bought all the surviving flyable Comet 4s during the late 1960s and into the 70s. Most were operated on the carrier's inclusive tour charters; a total of 48 Comets of all marks were owned by the Airline, making them the largest single operator of Comets.

The de Havilland Comet, the world's first jet airliner, evolved into the Hawker Siddeley Nimrod, a long range maritime patrol aircraft for the RAF that remained in service until 2011, over 60 years from the Comet's first flight.

Bristol Type 175 Britannia 312 G-AOVT

The final BOAC Britannia, 'VT also operated BOAC's first 'round the world' flight.

The British Airliner Collection's Britannia

'VT was the last of BOAC's Britannia 312 fleet to be delivered, arriving at Heathrow on 1st January 1959 after having its cabin furnishings and seats installed by Marshall of Cambridge. It operated on BOAC's long-range routes for more than four and a half years. In 1959 BOAC introduced the world's first round-the-world service with part being operated by Britannias and part by Comet 4s. 'VT operated the first of those westwards flights, flying via New York, San Francisco, Honolulu and Wake Island to Tokyo, from where a Comet 4 took over to complete the service by flying back to London with stops at Rangoon, Delhi and Rome.

It was donated to Duxford Aviation Society for preservation, and made its final flight to Duxford on 29th June 1975, the day when that year's airshow was being held, and landed during the flying display. It had then flown a total of 35,497 hours and made 10,760 landings.

A brief history

Known as the 'Whispering Giant' because of its extremely quiet engines, the Britannia was the world's first turbo-prop-powered large passenger transport aircraft. BOAC was the only customer for the Series 102 version and it received the first two of its order for 15 aircraft in December 1955. Engine intake icing problems delayed the Britannia 102's entry into service, but flights to Johannesburg eventually began on 1st December 1957. A stretched version of the Britannia was developed with three possible cabin configurations, (all passenger, mixed passenger and freight, or all-freight) and also long-range models with increased fuel capacity which enabled them to operate non-stop flights in both directions across the Atlantic. BOAC ordered 18 of the long range aircraft, designated Series 312s, and began services between London and New York on 19th December 1957.

When BOAC retired its Britannia 312s 'VT was purchased by British Eagle International Airlines in September 1963, and it was used on Eagle's inaugural internal UK services, and then on scheduled services and holiday charter and trooping flights until November 1968, when the airline ceased operations. 'VT was bought by the newly-formed Monarch Airlines in May 1969 and based at Luton Airport. It was used mainly on holiday package tour flights throughout Europe, but it also flew worldwide in various passenger and freight configurations, before operating the last civil passenger service by a Britannia in Europe on 14th October 1974, from Lisbon to Luton. 'VT's cabin was then stripped of all fittings and it was leased to Invicta Airlines at Manston who used it on cargo charter flights to Europe, Africa and the Middle East for three months. It returned to Luton on 10th March 1975 and was stored awaiting disposal.

Canadian Britannia Conversions

Long Range Maritime Patrol

The Canadair CP-107 Argus was a marine reconnaissance aircraft designed and manufactured by Canadair for the Royal Canadian Air Force. The Argus served throughout the Cold War in the RCAF's Maritime Air Command and later the CF's Maritime Air Group and Air Command.

Canadair began work on the Argus in April 1954 and at the time it was the largest aircraft built in Canada. The hybrid design was derived from the Bristol Britannia transport, having the same wings, tail surfaces and landing gear. The fuselage was completely redesigned by Canadair, going from the pressurised cabin of the Britannia to a non-pressurised one with bomb bays fore and aft of the wings. The powerplant was also changed from the Bristol Proteus turbo-prop engines to Wright R-3350 compound piston engines, which had lower fuel consumption necessary for extended missions over the sea.

Record Breaker

One of the most effective anti-submarine warfare aircraft of its day, the Argus was a mainstay for the RCAF. The aeroplane carried a great deal of equipment; including: search radar, sonar buoys, electronic counter measures and a magnetic anomaly detector. Up to 8,000lb of weapons could be carried in the bomb bays, including torpedoes, bombs, mines and depth charges.

A flight crew of five consisting of two pilots, a navigator, a flight engineer and a radio operator plus relief crew of four was normally carried. In addition, there were six or more ASW equipment operators depending on the mission requirements. The Argus had an endurance of approximately 26½ hours. An Argus flown by 407 Maritime Patrol Squadron held the record of slightly over 31 hours for the longest flight by an unrefuelled aircraft that stood for almost 20 years until broken by the Rutan Voyager experimental aircraft which circled the globe unrefuelled.

The stretched Britannia

The Canadair CL-44 was a turboprop airliner and cargo aircraft that was developed from Bristol Britannia and produced by Canadair in the late 1950s

The 'Whispering Giant' owed its quietness to the Bristol Proteus Turbo-prop; the company's first successful gas-turbine engine.

and early 1960s. Although innovative, only a small number of the aircraft were produced for commercial operators worldwide and for the Royal Canadian Air Force as the CC-106 Yukon.

The CL-44D4 was the first large aircraft to be able to 'swing' its tail, although some small naval aircraft had this feature to ease storage. It could be opened using hydraulic actuators to load large items quickly. An inflatable seal at the hinge-break enabled cabin pressure to be maintained, and eight hydraulic-operated locks assured structural integrity. It could be opened from controls within the tail in 90 seconds.

Loftleiðir was the only passenger operator of the CL-44J, a variant of the CL-44D4 stretched on request by Canadair. It was the largest passenger aircraft flying over the Atlantic at that time. Loftleiðir marketed the CL-44J under the name "Rolls-Royce 400 PropJet".

The forty-four proved to be a nightmare for mechanics. But it was an extremely profitable aircraft to run. At the time the fuel burn of a CL-44 was half compared to a Boeing 707.

After 40 years, out of the 39 built, 17 either crashed or were destroyed in operation. 19 aircraft have been cut up.

The remaining 3 aircraft are parked around the world or may have already been scrapped.

Not a single CL-44 has been preserved or found shelter in a museum unlike the British Airliner Collection's Britannia which is just one of several preserved airframes.

Handley Page HPR7 Dart Herald G-APWJ

This aircraft flew the last scheduled passenger service of the Herald, from Leeds to Belfast in 1985.

The British Aircraft Collection's Herald

Whiskey Juliet was built at the Handley Page factory at Radlett, Herts; the tenth Herald 201 off the production line. Its first flight took place on 29th May 1963. It had originally been ordered by Transair, but it was first registered to British United (Channel Island) Airways and was delivered to Jersey Airport on 13th June 1963.

On 1st November 1968 it was re-registered to British United Airways, and on 20th July 1970 it was re-

The HP Reading division
succeeded in producing a
modern design with
excellent flight and
performance characteristics.
However, the company made
a serious misjudgement
which was, in the end, to cost
the company dearly.

registered again, this time to British Island Airways, who operated it until January 1980, when it was re-registered to Air UK and based at Norwich.

Throughout its entire career 'WJ was used mainly on the short Blackpool, Isle of Man, and Channel Island routes and also routes to France, and during its 22 years in service it flew more than 33,000 hours in 44,000 flights and carried an estimated 2 million passengers a total of more than 6 million miles.

By 1985 'WJ was the only Herald being operated by Air UK, all of its others having been retired and replaced by Fokker F27 Friendships. 'WJ's final planned service was from Jersey to Southampton on 29th June 1985,

but it was unexpectedly forced back into service when one of Air UK's Friendships went unserviceable, and 'WJ was flown to Leeds to operate a service to Belfast, which was the very last scheduled passenger flight by a Herald.

'WJ was donated to the Duxford Aviation Society for preservation, and made its final flight from Norwich to Duxford on Sunday, 7th July 1985. It carried a full load of Air UK employees, and the flight took just 30 minutes.

This aircraft is currently undergoing major conservation work.

How the Herald got its Darts

(With apologies to Rudyard Kipling)

In the mid-1950s the Handley Page Aircraft Company proposed a new, fast, short-range regional airliner, intended to replace the venerable Douglas DC-3, particularly in third-world countries. The design, originally known as the HPR-3 Herald, emanated from the drawing office at Handley Page (Reading) Limited. The Herald was an extensive re-development of the original concept of the Miles Marathon, notable for its high mounted wing. The HP Reading division succeeded in producing a modern design with excellent flight and performance characteristics. However, the company made a serious misjudgement which was, in the end, to cost the company dearly.

Piston Power

After extensive consultation with DC-3 operators, it was decided to power the new airliner with piston engines, rather than the relatively new and untried turboprops, which were considered risky by the small airlines at which the Herald was aimed. Handley Page preferred a four engined design, which lead to the new 870 hp Alvis Leonides Major 14-cylinder radial engine, driving three-bladed propellers being chosen. At almost the same time, the Dutch company Fokker made the opposite choice for its competitor for the same market, choosing to power the F27 Friendship with two Rolls-Royce Darts.

At first, it seemed that Handley Page had made the right choices with the Herald. Extensive work by the sales team had produced considerable interest from potential customers, and Handley Page had 29 orders for the Herald by the time the first prototype made its maiden flight from Radlett on 25th August 1955, three months ahead of the first flight of the Friendship.

Viscount Success

By now, however, the Rolls-Royce Dart turboprop engine had shown proven success in the Vickers Viscount. Queensland Airlines and Australian National Airways cancelled their orders for Heralds in favour of turboprop-powered Friendships. Before the second prototype had been completed, Handley Page was faced with the fact that it had no orders for the Herald, and that the market had changed and wanted turboprops.

The Change

As there had already been a very substantial investment in the Herald project, Handley Page decided to press ahead with the project, in an effort to recover the investment; announcing a new version powered by the two Rolls-Royce Dart turboprops The revised aircraft, now designated the HPR.7 Dart Herald, was powered by 1,910 hp Dart 527 engines driving 12ft/3.8m variable pitch four-blade Dowty Rotol propellers, and the fuselage was lengthened by 20 in (50 cm). The first prototype was converted to Dart Herald standard, making its maiden flight on 11th March 1958.

The first proper order for the Dart Herald was in June 1959, some 4 years after the first flight, from British European Airways for three aircraft for use on its Scottish Highlands and Islands routes. The Herald, had by this time, lost its initial lead over the Friendship, which had entered service over six months previously.

The second prototype was converted to Series 200 standard and flew in that form on 8th April 1961. Jersey Airlines began operations with a leased Series 100 on 16th May 1961, receiving the first of its own Series 200s in January 1962, while BEA began Herald operations in March 1962.

Not Enough

The Herald attracted much early interest around the world because of its astonishing short field performance and excellent flight characteristics, but Handley Page failed to close many of the deals. While the Herald was cheap compared to its major competitors, and had a roomy cabin, the rival, and also Dart powered, Friendship could carry a larger payload and both it and the Avro 748 (Darts again) had superior performance which resulted in better long-term economics. By 1963, only 35 Heralds had been sold compared with over 240 Friendships. Unfortunately not even belated Rolls-Royce Darts could make the Herald attractive; and although it found work with several small operators it never achieved the success of the Friendship.

Vickers Super VC10 Type 1151 G-ASGC

BOAC's third Super VC10 and the star of its advertising campaign for 1965!

The British Airliner Collection's Super VC10

G-ASGC was built at Weybridge as the third of 17 Super VC10s ordered by BOAC in addition to its 12 Standard VC10s. 'GCs first flight on 1st January 1965 was a short one to the nearby BAC flight test centre at Wisley. It was flown to Shannon for crew training on 8th February, before being officially handed over to BOAC-Cunard on 27th March and delivered to Heathrow on 30th April. Four days later it entered service on the North Atlantic route. The BOAC-Cunard partnership was dissolved in 1966.

In 1972 BOAC became part of British Airways, and 'GC was later repainted in BA colours. BA began to

History and Development

withdraw its Super VC10s from service in 1979, and immediately prior to their retirement some were used on European routes for a time. 'GC's last commercial flight was from Amsterdam to London on 22nd October 1979 after which it was stored at Heathrow. 'GC was donated to the Duxford Aviation Society, and was flown to Duxford on 15th April 1980. Its landing here was its 16,415th, and it had flown a total of just under 54,623 hours.

The VC10 was built in two versions – the Standard VC10 and the larger Super VC10. 18 of the Standards and 22 Supers were built for use by airlines, and 14 C Mk 1s were supplied to the RAF for use by Transport Command as mixed passenger and freight aircraft, making a total of 54 built. The aircraft was very popular with passengers because of the low noise level due to its rear-mounted engines. A number of VC10s are still in service with the RAF.

The Super VC10 was a longer, more powerful and more economical version of the original VC10.

BOAC's position towards the VC10 changed many times. As the principle customer, BOAC wrote a specification that was so specific that the resultant aeroplane lost a lot of the flexibility in operations that could have meant a much larger order book and offer significant competition to Boeing and Douglas in America. That Vickers managed to deliver an aircraft that could cope with the specifications - and exceed them - is admirable but this view was not shared by the BOAC board. Even before the first VC10 had been delivered they were already complaining about its economics. This went so far that at one point they demanded a government subsidy for operating the type!

The major reason for developing the Super VC10 was the relatively high seat-mile costs of the Standard VC10 when compared to the main competitors. It did meet up to the specification that BOAC had put out, but at a cost. With the Super VC10 some of the 'hot-and-high' performance of the Standard was traded against a higher capacity, which made it a more economical aircraft. It was still a bit more costly than a 707 but a strange thing happened: the load factors of the VC10 turned out to be significantly higher than on the 707 fleet; a sure sign of its popularity.

The rear-engined layout made for a relatively quiet cabin and the efficient wings gave it a very smooth ride over turbulence. These qualities actually made passengers request the VC10 when given the choice, and BOAC used them to advantage when advertising with the phrases 'Swift, silent, superb' and 'A little VC10derness'. Pilots were also very appreciative of their new aircraft stating that it was a true 'pilot's aeroplane'.

The VC10 therefore featured heavily in many advertisements. The contrast between the complaints in the background and the virtues of the type shown in the advertising campaigns is striking.

One small plus of the VC10 that was not often mentioned was the fact that there was a separate toilet for use by the flight crew; on earlier types they sometimes used the "fasten seatbelts" signs to make sure that a toilet was available for crew use, but this was no longer needed on the VC10!

Hijack!

G-ASGR Dubai 21st November 1974

"On the evening of 21st November 1974 Captain Jim Futcher and his crew were at Dubai Airport awaiting the inbound flight from London to continue the BA870 schedule to the Far East. During the refuelling stop four men disguised as airport workers left the passenger lounge and ran towards the aircraft firing guns. A stewardess standing near the rear steps was hit but fortunately survived. On board they realised that the captain was not there and they demanded that he should get to the aeroplane or they would start shooting passengers.

Captain Futcher did not hesitate and made his way to the aircraft despite the airport's security officer urging him to stay out of sight. As he entered the aircraft he was met by a terrorist holding a gun to the head of a young New Zealander who greeted him with "Thanks for coming aboard Skipper". The aircraft took off with 27 passengers, 8 airport workers who had been cleaning the interior and 10 crew members.

As the authorities had closed off the airport at Beirut where the hijackers wanted to go to, the Super VC10 refuelled at Tripoli before landing at Tunis where it was surrounded by troops. The hijackers decided to stick to their demand for the release of 7 Palestinians held in Cairo and Holland. They set a deadline 24 hours away and promised to execute a passenger for every two hours past that time. When no progress was visible after 24 hours they murdered a German banker and dropped his body to the ground from the aft passenger door. Negotiations resulted in the Cairo-held hostages being brought to the plane in exchange for 7 hostages. When the other two prisoners from Holland arrived the remaining hostages were also released, leaving Captain Futcher, his co-pilot and flight engineer on board. Meanwhile the hijackers had been informed that their action had been condemned from all sides and their request for asylum in Tunis was also denied. Captain Futcher did his best to reason with them amidst their statements that they were willing to die for their cause. Time passed and deadlines went but the crew was still held inside the VC10 with various explosives set around the cockpit. After an ordeal totalling 84 hours a gunman came to the cockpit but instead of the message the crew was dreading he informed them that they had decided to surrender.

Captain Futcher was extensively recognised for his heroism in this case and awarded the Queen's Gallantry Medal. He passed away in 2008 aged 86."

Extract from Captain Futcher's obituary in the Daily Telegraph

THE BRITISH
AIRLINER COLLECTION

Hawker Siddeley H.S. 121 Trident 2E G-AVFB

The first airliner designed to be equipped with Blind Landing equipment to enable it to land in all weather conditions, including fog.

The British Airliner Collection's Trident

FB was the second of fifteen Trident 2Es ordered by BEA. It made its first flight at Hatfield on 2nd November 1967, and was delivered to Heathrow on 6th June 1968.

In June 1972 it was sold to Cyprus Airways, to replace one of that airline's 2Es which had been damaged in a heavy landing, and was re-registered 5B-DAC In July 1974.'AC was parked at Nicosia airport when the Turks invaded Northern Cyprus, and it suffered gunfire damage in the ensuing fighting. Afterwards it was abandoned on the airfield along with other damaged Tridents.

Eventually British Airways sent some engineers to survey the Tridents to see if any of them could be repaired and then recovered to London with a view to returning them to service. 'AC was in better condition than the other aircraft, having sustained just some bullet holes in its fuselage, and these were repaired

with patches. It was ferried to Heathrow in May 1977, and restored to its original British registration. Following its total refurbishment and repainting in BA livery, 'FB was used on the airline's inter-city shuttle services until 27th March 1982, when it operated a London-Manchester service. It was then donated to the DAS, and was flown to Duxford on 13th June 1982, where the year's main airshow was being held, and performed a short display before landing. It had then flown a total of 21,642 hours and made 11,726 landings. Work then began to prepare the aircraft for opening to the public. In 1990 'FB was repainted in its original BEA 'Red Square' livery. Since then the Trident has remained on display outside, and this has necessitated a continual programme of monitoring both its external and internal condition and dealing with any problems that are encountered.

History and Development

The Hawker Siddeley Trident was the first aircraft to be designed from the outset to be equipped with Blind Landing equipment as standard to enable it to land in all weather conditions, including fog. It was also designed specifically to meet the needs of British European Airways, but the airline made so many changes to its specification during the design stages that the first model, the Trident 1, was too small and had too limited a passenger-carrying capacity and range to appeal to other European airlines. In an attempt to remedy this, the larger and more powerful Trident 2 series, and then the even bigger Trident 3 series were produced.

Three unique Trident facts

The Trident is probably best known as the aeroplane that pioneered the 'blind' landing system, of which more below, but among aficionados it is also known as the predecessor of the Boeing 727; had it not been so closely tailored to BEAs ever changing demands it too may have enjoyed the commercial success of its American rival.

Apart from taking thousands of us on holiday in the 70s and 80s it is particularly remembered for the three facts below.

Speed

The Trident was one of the fastest subsonic commercial airliners, regularly cruising at over 610 mph (965 km/h). At introduction into service its standard cruising speed was 580 mph, the highest of any of its contemporaries. Designed for high speed, the wing produced relatively limited lift at lower speeds. This, and the aircraft's low power-to-weight ratio, called for prolonged take-off runs. Nevertheless, the Trident fulfilled BEA's 6,000 ft (1,800 m) field length criterion and its relatively staid airfield performance was deemed adequate.

Reverse Thrust Prior to Touchdown

The Trident was routinely able to descend at rates of up to 4500 fpm (23 m/sec) in regular service. In emergency descents it was permissible to use reverse thrust of up to 10,000 rpm. Below 28okt IAS (Indicated Air Speed), it was also possible to extend the main landing gear for use as an emergency airbrake. The Trident's first version, Trident 1C, had the unusual capability of using reverse thrust prior to touchdown. The throttles could be closed in the flare and reverse idle set to open the reverser buckets. At pilot discretion, up to full reverse thrust could then be used prior to touchdown.

Autoland and the 'moving map'

The Trident's advanced avionics displayed the aircraft's momentary position relative to the ground on a moving map display on the centre instrument panel. This electro-mechanical device also recorded the aircraft's track using a stylus plotting on a motor-driven paper map. Positional information was derived from a Doppler navigation system which read groundspeed and drift data which, alongside heading data, drove the stylus.

The Trident had a complex, sophisticated and comprehensive avionics fit which was successful in service. This comprised a completely automatic blind landing system developed by Hawker Siddeley and Smiths Aircraft Instruments. It was capable of guiding the aircraft automatically during airfield approach, flare, touchdown and even roll-out from the landing runway. The system was intended to offer autoland by 1970. In the event, it enabled the Trident to perform the first automatic landing by a civil airliner in scheduled passenger service as early as 10th June 1965 and the first genuinely "blind" landing in scheduled passenger service as early as 4th November 1966.

The ability to land in fog solved a major problem at London Heathrow and other British airports. Because the Trident fleet could operate safely to airfields equipped with suitable ILS (Instrument Landing System) installations, it could operate as scheduled irrespective of weather, while other aircraft were forced to divert.

In Conclusion

Subsequently autoland systems became available on a number of aircraft types but the primary customers were those mainly European airlines whose networks were severely affected by radiation fog. In America it was generally the case that reduced but not zero visibility was often associated with these conditions, and if the visibility really became almost zero in, for example, blowing snow or other precipitation then operations would be impossible for other reasons. As a result neither airlines nor airports placed a high priority on operations in the lowest visibility. The provision of the necessary ground equipment (ILS) and associated systems for Category 3 operations was almost non-existent and the major manufacturers did not regard it as a basic necessity for new aircraft.

This led to the absurd situation for British Airways that, as the launch customer for the Boeing 757 to replace the Trident, the brand-new "advanced" aircraft had inferior all weather operations capability compared to the fleet being broken up for scrap. An indication of this philosophical divide is the comment from a senior Boeing Vice President that he could not understand why British Airways were so concerned about the Category 3 certification, as there were only at that time two or three suitable runways in North America on which it could be fully used. It was pointed out that British Airways had some 12 such runways on its domestic network alone, four of them at its main base at Heathrow!

BAC One-Eleven Series 510ED G-AVMU

The Last All-British Jet Airliner

The British Airliner Collection's BAC 1-11

G-AVMU was one of 18 BAC 1-11 type 510EDs ordered by BEA, the launch customer for the stretched Series 500 version of the very successful 1-11 twin jet airliner.

It made its first flight on 19th January 1969, and was delivered to BEA on 19th March of that year.

BEA based its 1-11 500s at Birmingham Airport, from where they operated services throughout Europe, including internal German Services to Berlin. During a landing there its undercarriage was damaged, but repairs were carried out, and 'MU continued to operate on BEA services until the airline became part of the newly-formed British Airways in April 1972. When BA gave most of its aircraft fleets names, 'MU was named "County of Dorset".

'MU was eventually withdrawn when BA retired its 1-11 510s and they were all flown to Hurn airport, and stored awaiting disposal, with their BA titles painted over. It was eventually selected for preservation and donated to Duxford Aviation Society, and made its final flight to Duxford on 4th March 1993. It had then flown a total of 40,279 hours and made 45,540 landings.

History and Development

BEA/British Airways 500 series aircraft (denoted 1-11 510ED) varied significantly from other 1-11s, at BEA's request. The One-Eleven 510ED had a modified cockpit which incorporated instrumentation and avionics from or similar to that of the Hawker Siddeley HS.121 Trident, for better commonality with the type. Their additional equipment included a more sophisticated autoflight system, which allowed CAT II autolandings and included an autothrottle. The modifications went as far as reversing the "on"

position of most switches to match that of the Trident; indeed, the 510ED was so different from other One-Elevens and 500 series aircraft that a different type rating was required to fly it.

Reliable and safe

BAC1-11; the last all-British jet (airframe and engine) was only exceeded by the Viscount in numbers sold but in value easily surpassed it.

It led the way in a two crew cockpit for jet airliners which of course has now become standard. In BEA service they were thrown straight into the Berlin-Tempelhof services from new, flying up to twelve sectors a day with twenty minute turnarounds with a degree of technical and operational reliability unknown before. With BEA/BA the type flew over a million hours without a single passenger fatality.

The Flying Testbed

> The BAC 1-11 airframe was probably the strongest ever built on an airliner. In the Philippines, two BAC 1-11's suffered in-flight bombs and both landed safely.
>
> MICHAEL BRETT.

Military Marks and Testing Times

A further testament to the 1-11's durability was its use as a test aircraft at Boscombe Down, home to what is now QinetiQ. When the first aircraft came on strength, this state owned organisation was known as the Royal Aircraft Establishment (RAE), becoming QinetiQ in 2001.

The first BAC One-Eleven to adopt military marks in the United Kingdom was a Series 201AC which was purchased from Caledonian//BUA in April 1971 and was delivered to the Blind Landing Experimental Unit (BLEU) at RAE Bedford (Thurleigh), Bedfordshire as XX105 on 26th March 1973. This was to be the first of five One-Elevens to eventually carry military serials in the United Kingdom and was fitted with long range tanks and specialist radar prior to delivery. Apart from its autoland tests, it was also used to trial civil and military avionics systems. The aircraft was relocated to Farnborough on 23rd March 1994 and onwards to Boscombe Down on 23rd August of the same year. It was later fitted with a coloured 'glass' cockpit and had touch screen flying controls added during the latter part of its life. It was moved to the Boscombe Down Aviation Collection where it remained until October 2010 when it was removed for scrapping.

In the late spring of 1984 the two Series 400s of Air Pacific were obtained. The first became ZE433 and was based at Thurleigh where it was converted into a flying laboratory. Initially operated in basic Air Pacific colours without titles, it later adopted the famous RAE red, white and blue 'Raspberry Ripple' colour scheme. The nose was modified and extended to accommodate the Blue Vixen airborne interception radar for in flight trials. This new radar was due to be installed in the Sea Harrier FA2.

Following the completion of these trials, the aircraft was further modified to accept the ECR90 radar that was due to be used in the Eurofighter Typhoon. It first flew in this form on 8th January 1993 and incorporated ram air and liquid cooling systems fitted in the forward hold for equipment cooling. Accommodation was provided for four Flight Observers on sliding/swivel seats facing starboard to monitor the equipment installed. Fourteen seats at the rear of the cabin were provided for additional observers with intercom facilities.

This aircraft was put into storage after performing its last flight into Boscombe Down on 13th November 2008. It is presently being used for spares.

The second aircraft was taken over by the Empire Test Pilots' School as ZE432 and initially painted in the same 'Raspberry Ripple' colour scheme as its sister ship with 'Empire Test Pilots' School' titles. Training stations were installed in the forward cabin while the standard Air Pacific seating and overhead racks were retained to the rear. It was withdrawn from service during November 2009 due to major corrosion issues.

And finally:

As a testament to the strength of the airframe the history of Philippine Airlines RP-C1184 cannot be bettered. This aircraft had a bomb explode in the rear toilet in flight on two separate occasions blowing off part of the cabin roof each time but survived both incidents to fly again. Neither bomber survived!

BAC / Aerospatiale Concorde 101 G-AXDN

The fastest ever Concorde and the single most popular exhibit at the museum

The British Airliner Collection's Concorde

This aircraft was originally designated Concorde 01, later changed to 101. It had been announced in Parliament that the aircraft would be donated to the Duxford Aviation Society by the then Department of Industry when its test flying days were over, and it remained in a hangar at Filton awaiting its delivery to Duxford. Filton were preoccupied with assembling Concordes for British Airways, and pressure had to be applied to get them to prepare 01 for its final flight, as construction work on the M11 motorway was getting ever closer to Duxford, and a quarter of the runway was due to be dug up to accommodate the new road. 01 was eventually flown to Duxford on Saturday, 20th August 1977 and just two days later, on Monday the 22nd, the motorway builders began work to shorten the runway.

History and Development

101 is the British pre-production version of Concorde, and the third Concorde built. It was assembled at the British Aircraft Corporation factory at Filton, Bristol, and was larger and of a more advanced design than the two prototypes, the French-built 001 and the British built 002 which both made their first flights in 1969, some 20 months before 101 first flew. 101's fuselage was 8ft 6ins longer, and it had a completely new nose section which incorporated a fully transparent visor to replace the metal ones fitted to the prototypes, which were not popular with the pilots and would not have been certificated by the American FAA because they provided very poor forward and downward vision in supersonic flight. The new-profile nose section with the transparent visor was designed by Marshall of Cambridge. 101 is unique in being the only Concorde built with a 193 foot long fuselage, as all seventeen Concordes built after it had fuselages some nine feet longer, the rear fuselage having been extended aft of the tail fin, which provided less drag which in turn resulted in an improved performance.

101 was rolled out on 20th September 1971, and its first flight on 17th December was from Filton to Fairford, where the BAC Concorde Flight Test centre was located until January 1977. Its main contribution to the Concorde test programme was in the proving of the engine variable intake control system, arguably the most important single piece of equipment on Concorde that enabled it to fly supersonically. When Concorde was flying at its cruising speed of just over twice the speed of sound (1,350mph) the air entering the engines had to be slowed down to around 500mph in the 11ft long intake by computer-controlled adjustable ramps, as no air-breathing engine can accept air entering it at supersonic speed.

In the course of testing the system 101 visited Tangier twice, and during the second visit in March 1974 it achieved Mach 2.23, or approximately 1,450mph, at an altitude of 63,700ft, the highest speed recorded by any Concorde.

In November of the same year 01 flew from Fairford to Bangor, Maine, in 2 hours 56 minutes, a record time for a commercial aircraft flying across the Atlantic in a Westerly direction. Here it spent a month carrying out flights to prove the efficiency of the airframe electrical de-icing system, which had to be capable of melting off any accumulated ice up to two inches thick. For these tests areas of the fuselage and the port wing surface were painted black to show up ice, and miniature television cameras were fitted in various positions on the aircraft's exterior and a monitoring screen was set up in its cabin area so that an operator could view the aircraft's exterior during flight. 101 made a total of 11 flights from Moses Lake in search for weather cold enough to produce the required thickness of ice, and on 4th December it finally succeeded. With this particular test programme completed 101 returned to Fairford on 13th December, recording the same flight time from Bangor as it did for the outward flight.

101's achievements and the records which it set during its test flying are recorded in the artwork on its port-side forward fuselage.

The remainder of 101's flying career was spent at Fairford testing modifications designed to give airline Concordes improved performance and range. Its contribution to the Concorde flight test development programme ended on 16th May 1975, and it was then used for the training of BAC flight crews whose job it was to instruct the British Airways pilots and flight engineers prior to the start of Concorde commercial services in January 1976. 101 remained at Fairford until the Test Centre eventually closed, and it was flown back to Filton.

101 spent almost 20 years of its time at Duxford on display outside, and became a familiar landmark for people driving on the M11 and the A505. It was first opened to the public in March 1978 and has been the most popular single exhibit at the Imperial War Museum, Duxford ever since, with an estimated four

million visitors having walked through it. It was eventually moved into what was Hangar 1 in late 1998, and remained there until it was moved out when work began in 2005 to extend the building and create what is now the AirSpace building. 101 was the second aircraft to be positioned in the new building in mid-2006. The aircraft is normally open to the public every day that the museum is open, and it provides visitors with a fascinating insight into the technical innovation that enabled airline passengers to enjoy supersonic flights from January 1976 until Concorde's eventual retirement in 2003.

A Concorde Pilot's Reminiscence

Concorde was once described as a piece of twentieth-century sculpture. That is a very apt description; she was truly a fusion of art and technology. She was an aeroplane that commanded attention, an aeroplane that one felt compelled to look at and admire for her beauty and grace. She transcended mere technology, inspiring a fierce loyalty and pride amongst all who were privileged to work with her. Concorde was not only beautiful to look at; she was also beautiful to fly. Concorde really was an aircraft that lived up to the adage that "if she looks right, she will fly right".

It is worth remembering that this is an aeroplane whose design technology goes back to the late 1950s and 1960s. The aerodynamicists and engineers who created her were a remarkable group of people who were far ahead of their time. It is eloquent testimony to their genius in overcoming the problems of supersonic flight that we are now in the twenty-first century and there is still no sign of a second-generation supersonic transport anywhere on the horizon. I am sure that it will come but we are probably going to have to wait for another twenty to thirty years.

I spent fifteen years flying Concorde and, out of all the seventy-plus types I have flown, I rate her as the most outstanding. She was a powerful and extremely responsive thoroughbred that could be flown with finger and thumb. Her handling qualities were superb throughout the whole speed range. From landing speeds of around 160 knots to cruising at Mach 2, twice the speed of sound, she was a sheer delight to fly and she did so effortlessly. The only clue when going through the sound barrier was the Mach meter going from 0.99 to 1.01 Mach and a fluctuation of the rate of climb indicator as the shock wave attached on the nose.

It is impossible to convey in words the sensation of supersonic flight but I will try. When cruising at 50,000ft up to her ceiling of 60,000ft one was above all the jet streams and thunderstorms. In that calm and tranquil environment on the edge of space one had no impression of speed. It felt as though one was hanging suspended in space waiting for Mother Earth to spin around and for the destination to appear below. The curvature of the earth was clearly visible at those heights and the colour of the sky took on a deep midnight blue. Only when flying over subsonic aircraft 20,000ft below did one get any feeling of speed; the subsonics would appear to be going backwards as Concorde overtook them, flying some 800mph faster!

The tragic crash at Paris left an unjustified blemish on her reputation and was the catalyst that led to the premature grounding of this truly special aircraft. If that tragedy had not occurred, she would still have been flying today and continuing to grace the skies until around 2020. Sadly there is no turning back of clocks and it will be several decades before air passengers can enjoy the great benefits of supersonic flight again.

In summary, Concorde was an aviation icon; the supreme achievement of passenger flight. People never talked about "the" Concorde or "a" Concorde. She was simply Concorde; the ultimate flying experience.

Captain John Hutchinson, Retired, British Airways

Aircraft Specifications

Avro York

Crew: 5
(two pilots, navigator, wireless operator, cabin steward)
Capacity: 56 passengers
Payload: 20,000 lb (9,100 kg)
Length: 78 ft 6 in (23.9 m)
Wingspan: 102 ft 0 in (31.1 m)
Height: 16 ft 6 in (5 m)
Wing area: 1,297 sq ft (120.5 sq m)
Empty weight: 40,000 lb (18,150 kg)
Loaded weight: 65,000 lb (29,480 kg)
Powerplant: 4 × Rolls-Royce Merlin 24 liquid-cooled V12 engines, 1,280 hp (950 kW) each
Maximum speed: 298 mph (479 km/h) at 21,000 ft (6,400 m)
Range: 3,000 mi (4,800 km)
Service ceiling: 23,000 ft (7,010 m)

De Havilland Dove Series 5

Crew: 2
Capacity: 8 passengers
Length: 39 ft 3 in (11.96 m)
Wingspan: 57 ft 0 in (17.37 m)
Height: 13 ft 4 in (4.06 m)
Wing area: 335 sq ft (31.1 sq m)
Empty weight: 5,725 lb (2,600 kg)
Loaded weight: 8,800 lb (4,000 kg)
Powerplant: 2 × de Havilland Gipsy Queen 70 Mk.2 geared, supercharged 6-cylinder in-line inverted air-cooled engine, 380 bhp (283 kW) each
Maximum speed: 202 mph at 8,000 ft (325 km/h at 2,400 m)
Range: 1,070 mi (1,720 km)
Service ceiling: 20,000 ft (6,100 m)

Handley Page Hermes IV

Crew: 7
Capacity: 40 - 82 passengers
Length: 96 ft 10 in (29.52 m)
Wingspan: 113 ft 0 in (34.45 m)
Height: 30 ft 0 in (9.15 m)
Wing area: 1,408.0 sq ft (130.85 sq m)
Empty weight: 55,350 lb (25,159 kg)
Max takeoff weight: 86,000 lb (39,092 kg)
Powerplant: 4 × Bristol Hercules 763 radial engines, 2,100 hp (1,566 kW) each
Maximum speed: 350 mph (567 km/h)
Cruise speed: 270 mph (437 km/h) at 20,000 ft
Range: 2,000 mi (3,242 km) with 14,125 lb (6,420 kg) payload
Service ceiling: 24,500 ft (7,470 m)

Airspeed Ambassador

Crew: 3
Capacity: Up to 60 passengers
Length: 82 ft 0 in (24.99 m)
Wingspan: 115 ft 0 in (35.05 m)
Height: 18 ft 10 in (5.74 m)
Wing area: 1,200 sq ft (111.48 sq m)
Empty weight: 35,377 lb (16,047 kg)
Loaded weight: 52,500 lb (23,814 kg)
Powerplant: 2 × Bristol Centaurus 661 two-row sleeve-valve radial piston engine, 2,625 hp (1,958 kw) each
Cruise speed: 260 mph (418 km/h)
Range: 550 mi (885km)

Vickers Viscount

Crew: Two pilots + cabin crew
Capacity: 75 passengers
Length: 85 ft 8 in (26.11 m)
Wingspan: 93 ft 8 in (28.56 m)
Height: 26 ft 9 in (8.15 m)
Wing area: 963 sq ft (89 sq m)
Empty weight: 41,276 lb (18,722 kg)
Max takeoff weight: 67,500 lb (30,617 kg)
Powerplant: 4 × Rolls-Royce Dart RDa.7/1 Mk 525 turboprop, 1,990hp (1,484 kW) each
Maximum speed: 352 mph (566 km/h)
Range: 1,380 mi (2,220 km)
Service ceiling: 25,000 ft (7,620 m)

De Havilland Comet 4

Crew: 4
(2 pilots, flight engineer and radio operator/navigator)
Capacity: 56–81 passengers 119 passengers could be accommodated in a special "charter seating" package in the later 4C series
Length: 111 ft 6 in (33.99 m)
Wingspan: 114 ft 10 in (35.00 m)
Height: 29 ft 6 in (8.99 m)
Wing area: 2,121 sq ft (197 sq m)
Empty weight: 75,400 lb (34,200 kg)
Max takeoff weight: 162,000 lb (73,500kg)
Powerplant: 4 × Rolls-Royce Avon Mk 524 turbojets, 10,500 lbf (46.8 kN) each
Maximum speed: 526 mph (846 km/h)
Range: 3,225 mi (5,190 km) (with 16,800 lb (7,620 kg) payload)
Service ceiling: 42,000 ft (12,800 m)